# PROCESS THEC
# CELTIC WIS~~~

## ADVENTURES IN ECOLOGICAL SPIRITUALITY

BRUCE G. EPPERLY

Topical Line Drives
Volume 31

Energion Publications
Gonzalez, Florida
2018

Unless otherwise annotated, scripture quotations are from the New Revised Standard Version of the Bible (NRSV), copyright © 1989 by the Division of the Christian Education of the National Council of the Churches of Christ in the USA.

Unless otherwise noted, Celtic prayers are adapted from multiple sources by the author.

ISBN10: 1-63199-619-3
ISBN13: 978-1-63199-619-1

Energion Publications
P. O. Box 841
Gonzalez, FL 32560

energion.co
pubs@energion.com

# TABLE OF CONTENTS

# CHAPTER ONE

## FINDING OUR PLACE OF RESURRECTION

According to Celtic spirituality, every journey should begin with a prayer. The path upon which we travel is filled with challenges and possibilities and danger lurks in the shadows. We need God's guidance and protection to find our way. Centuries ago, according to some legends, in a time of threat, St. Patrick, circled himself turning toward the sunrise as he said this prayer;

*I arise today*
*Through the strength of heaven;*
*Light of the sun,*
*Splendor of fire,*
*Speed of lightning,*
*Swiftness of the wind,*
*Depth of the sea,*
*Stability of the earth,*
*Firmness of the rock.*
*I arise today*
*Through God's strength to pilot me;*
*God's might to uphold me,*
*God's wisdom to guide me,*
*God's eye to look before me,*
*God's ear to hear me,*
*God's word to speak for me,*
*God's hand to guard me,*
*God's way to lie before me,*
*God's shield to protect me,*
*God's hosts to save me*
*Near and far,*
*Alone or in a multitude.*

Other Celtic Christian adventurers embarked on the high seas in little boats, known as coracles, without rudders to guide them, trusting that God's providence would lead them to their place of

1

resurrection, the holy ground upon which they would realize their destiny as God's companions in sharing the Gospel. While such sojourns were not the norm for Celtic pilgrims, now more than ever we need the witness of Celtic Christianity to respond to our current spiritual, theological, congregational, political, and ecological uncertainties. We travel the high seas of spiritual and cultural adventure, uncertain of our destination and buffeted by the waves of postmodernism, religious pluralism, ecological destruction, political polarization, and institutional collapse. Our little boats of faith are in danger of capsizing if we do not locate theological, spiritual, and ethical polestars to guide our journeys.

Celtic Christian theology and spirituality is undergoing a revival as a spiritual pathway uniquely suited to guide our way toward spiritual and planetary wholeness. Celtic Christianity presents a life-transforming vision of an enchanted reality, in which God speaks to us in the waves, songs of birds, groves of trees, and cries of newborn babies. The disenchanted worldview, propagated by Western religion, economics, and politics alienated humankind from the non-human world, made earth and sea a garbage dump, and threatens the survival of the planet. Political and business leaders have jettisoned the wisdom of the prophets to achieve short term profits. Among many Christians, the doctrine of original sin turns our attention from earth to heaven, devalues the non-human world, and inspires apocalyptic scenarios in which God is the ultimate destroyer and humans have no agency in saving the planet.

The revival of Celtic spirituality has been an antidote to the destructive impact of "orthodox" doctrines original sin, divine wrath, predestination, and evangelism. Grounded in ancient wisdom, well-suited to seacoast villages and verdant countryside, the enchanted world view of Celtic Christianity needs to be complemented and expanded by reenchanted philosophical and theological visions such as those characterizing process theology. Grounded in an appreciation of the scientific adventure and technological achievement, process theology offers a vision of an interdependent, creation-affirming spirituality, inspired by the movements of a dynamic, relational, creative, and freedom loving God.

This text joins Celtic spiritual wisdom with process theology to nurture an earth-affirming faith for a pluralistic, postmodern, experience-oriented, and iconoclastic age. We need a faith that is spacious enough to embrace the multi-billion-year universe adventure, our planet's evolutionary journey, and the wondrous ethnic, racial, cultural, sexual, and religious diversity of humankind. While this short text cannot fully answer life's deepest questions, its goal is to provide a theological and spiritual GPS to orient our personal, congregational, and planetary pilgrimages.

The chapters that follow will be meditative in spirit, capturing the vision of Celtic spirituality and process theology and connecting them to the key spiritual and cultural issues of the twenty-first century. This is not just an academic exercise, unrelated to today's planetary and national crises; it is intensely pastoral and practical. Our visions of reality guide our personal and cultural journeys and can be a matter of life and death for the human and non-human world. Despite our affluence and technological accomplishments, the path we have been traveling is leading us toward ecological destruction and social chaos. We need to re-orient our spiritual and theological GPS to find more healthy pathways to the future, supportive of human agency in the context of our amazing, but fragile, planet. Accordingly, as we begin our spiritual journey, let us seek God's creative wisdom as we encircle ourselves in holy wisdom and awaken to divine guidance with a Celtic prayer;

*Bless, O Bless, Thou God of grace,*
*Each day and hour of my life.*
*God bless the pathway on which I go,*
*God bless the earth that is beneath my sole;*
*Bless, O God, and give to me Thy love.*[1]

---

1    de Waal, *The Celtic Way of Prayer* (New York: Image Books, 1999), 90.

## CHAPTER TWO

### REENCHANTING THE WORLD: CELTIC WISDOM FOR THE TWENTY-FIRST CENTURY

Can we reclaim as a culture the enchanted realities our first parents felt as they gazed at the heavens or the enchantment a young child feels as she follows the path of a butterfly across her backyard? Can we once again embrace each moment, "trailing clouds of glory," as the poet William Wordsworth imagines? This morning, as I meandered on the Cape Cod beach near my home, bathing my senses in the scudding clouds, chill breeze, sea air, and rhythm of waves, I felt the spirit of the Celtic voyagers as one of their prayers guided my steps:

> *God of the love of skies be thine*
> *God of the love of stars be thine*
> *God of the love of moon be thine*
> *God of the love of seas be thine...*
> *Power of the storm be thine*
> *Power of moon be thine.*
> *Power of sun.*
> *Power of sea be thine*
> *Power of land be thine.*
> *Power of heaven.*
> *Thine be the might of river*
> *Thine be the might of ocean*
> *Thine be the might of the love on high.*[2]

Centuries before my sunrise walk, the Celtic spiritual guide whose words inspired my steps might have been thinking of the Psalmist's hymn of praise:

---

2 Adapted from the Carmina Gaedelica III, 231. Quoted in J. Phillip Newell, *The Book of Creation: An Introduction to Celtic Spirituality* (Mahweh, NY: Paulist Press, 1999), 22-23.

*Praise the LORD!*
*Praise the LORD from the heavens;*
*praise God in the heights!*
*Praise God , all angels;*
*praise God, all heavenly host!*
*Praise God, sun and moon;*
*praise God, all you shining stars!*
*Praise God, you highest heavens,*
*and you waters above the heavens!*
*Praise the LORD from the earth,*
*you sea monsters and all deeps,*
*fire and hail, snow and frost,*
*stormy wind fulfilling his command!*
*Mountains and all hills,*
*fruit trees and all cedars!*
*Wild animals and all cattle,*
*creeping things and flying birds!*
*Kings of the earth and all peoples,*
*princes and all rulers of the earth!*
*Young men and women alike,*
*old and young together!*
*Let everything that breathes praise God!*
*Praise God!* (Psalm 148:1-4, 7-11; Psalm 150:6)[3]

Many modern Christians have forgotten the enchanted reality of scripture. We have portrayed God as a distant, coercive power, whose word and will separate humankind from lifeless nature. Following the image of a unilateral, arbitrary, and domineering God, we have interpreted the Genesis call to dominion in terms of domination and destruction. We have turned away from the biblical vision of the goodness of creation, humanity's embeddedness in the non-human world, and our vocation as God's agents of Shalom. While the legendary "fall of humankind" may have eventuated in separation from nature, our calling as God's beloved children is to repair the breach and mend the world, by using our intelligence and power to bring healing and beauty to the earth. The One who

---

3    I have substituted "God" for "him" throughout the text.

rejoiced in God's presence in lilies, birds, and children, invites us to experience God's wise creativity and love in all things.

Celtic spirituality invites us to reenchant the universe and our daily lives. The theology of the Celtic Christians is far from abstract or unworldly. It emerged in the context of voyages, pilgrimages, and interactions with the native Druids. Life was wild, sometimes precarious, and always adventurous for these Celtic pilgrims. A "theospirituality" emerged in which theological reflection is profoundly earth-affirming and practical and intimately connected with mystic visions that join the quest for salvation and wholeness with the freshness of life, the star-filled heavens, the rolling waves, and the amazing beauty of human and non-human creation.

As I reflect on Celtic wisdom, I believe that its spiritual vision is best understood in terms of a loosely-gathered collection of lively affirmations that shape our experiences of the world rather than rigid doctrines to which we must adhere to be considered among the faithful. These affirmations inspire a earth-affirming, green spirituality and ethic.

*First, Celtic Christianity affirms that we live on a beautiful planet, wild, wonderful, and constantly shaped by divine wisdom.* As the apostle Paul affirms, God is the reality within which "we live and move and have our being" (Acts 17:28). A few weeks ago, one of my young grandchildren gazed at the sky and exclaimed, "That's Orion's belt!" Last night, a Nor'easter blew across Cape Cod, gusty winds shook our house, downed powerlines, and propelled us back two centuries as we lit candles and huddled under the covers. In the midst of the storm, I visualized the ancient Hebrews and their Celtic followers imagining God riding the wind and waves, as they chanted, "power of storm be thine, power of sea be thine." Our planet is the temple of God, revealing "God's grandeur," as Gerard Manley Hopkins rejoices, in every plant, flying bird, breaching whale, and human face. God is in the storm at sea and the calm that follows. God guides the world process toward beauty, apart from human interests. As another Celtic prayer affirms, "I am the wind that breathes upon the sea, I am the wave on the ocean."[4]

---

4    Robert Van de Weyer, *Celtic Fire* (London: Darton, Longman, and Todd, 1990), 92.

With Jewish theologian and mystic, Abraham Joshua Heschel, we can affirm that the heart of religious experience is radical amazement at the very fact of existence and the intricate beauty and wisdom bursting forth in galaxies, dolphins at play, and a mother giving birth.

*Second, the Celtic sages affirmed that humankind is created in God's image as God's beautiful and beloved children.* In contrast to the spiritually-debilitating and creation-destroying Augustinian and "orthodox" Roman and Protestant doctrine of original sin, Celtic Christianity proclaims the original goodness and beauty of life. Pelagius, condemned as a heretic by orthodoxy, affirmed the deepest truth of our nature in the words: when we gaze at a newborn, we see the face of God. Sin is real and obvious in the bloviations of political leaders, school shootings and the failure of our nation to enact laws that protect children rather than guns and the realities of sexual harassment and abusive behavior, the growing gap between the rich and poor, the destruction of the ecosystem, and our own imperfection and apathy at the crises we face. But, sin is derivative, and not primary. The world is created in wisdom and beauty, the light shines everywhere, and the darkness of sin cannot conquer it (John 1:5). God says to every child the words that God said to Jesus at His baptism: "You are my child, my beloved; with you I am well pleased" (Mark 1:11, AP).

*Third, Celtic Christianity believes that God loves the non-human world.* One of my grandsons once asked, "Does God love sharks?" In reflecting on John 3:16, "for God so loved the world," the answer is unreservedly "yes." Our separation and devaluation of the non-human world has led to our earth becoming what Pope Francis describes as a garbage dump. Whatever God creates, God loves, and God has patiently brought forth a world of variety and wonder, whose every creature, plant, wave, and rock formation reveals divine creative wisdom. We are surely not the only intelligent life on our planet: behold the chirping of dolphins, the songs of humpbacked whales, the pain elephants experience at the loss of their partner, the loyalty and love of a dog for his companion person, the patience and craftiness of the crow, and the gentle beauty of the blue whale swimming across the sea. Every cell is alive in

7

wonder, and plants, trees, and water crystals respond to health or illness in their environments. Apart from human interest and financial profit, nature is good because it is God's creation, and beloved by its Creator, who delights in its manifold wonder. Within the non-human world is both joy and suffering, and the desire, albeit at a different level than ours, for life in all its abundance.

*Fourth, Celtic spirituality recognizes that we are all connected.* The Celts affirmed the holiness of relationships. In the spirit of African wisdom of *ubuntu*, "I am because of you," the Celtics delighted in spiritual friendships (*anamcara*) and asserted that a person without a spiritual friend is like a ship without a rudder. The Celts knew that no one is self-made. Despite their fierce independence, the Celts equally prized interdependence, not only with the human community but with the non-human world that supports us and provides for our needs. Within the Body of Christ – and this surely goes beyond the institutional church or Christianity – no part can exist alone and every part has an impact on the whole creature. "If one member suffers, all suffer together with it; if one member is honored, all rejoice together with it" (I Corinthians 12:31; see I Corinthians 12:1-31).

*Fifth, Celtic Christians believe that God's wisdom and energy are present everywhere and in all things.* An ancient sage affirmed that "God is a circle whose center is everywhere and whose circumference is nowhere." Celtic Christianity affirms the omnipresence and omni-activity of God. Wherever our path takes us, God is with us. When we go to sleep God's love surrounds us and inspires us with dreams. When we are lost, God makes a way through the wilderness. When we ask, God will respond. In times of challenge, we can affirm in the spirit of the Prayer of St. Patrick:

> *Christ with me, Christ before me, Christ behind me,*
> *Christ in me, Christ beneath me, Christ above me,*
> *Christ on my right, Christ on my left,*
> *Christ when I lie down, Christ when I sit down,*
> *Christ in the heart of everyone who thinks of me,*
> *Christ in the mouth of everyone who speaks of me,*
> *Christ in the eye that sees me,*
> *Christ in the ear that hears me.*

God's ambient love surrounds and guides us, illuminating our path through the shadows of uncertainty and human-made chaos.

*Sixth, Celtic pilgrims affirm that God's revelation and salvation is global in scope and personal in nature.* The Celtic Christian spirit was profoundly influenced by the creation stories of Genesis and John's Gospel. A good creation reveals holiness in every cell and soul. The original wholeness of humankind and the non-human world makes each place a potential "thin place" where the divinity and creation are joined in a dance of creative beauty. Each moment brings revelation. Each child's birth brings new beauty to the planet. Each culture and every faith tradition have gifts of wisdom and healing from which we can learn. As John's Gospel proclaims, "The true light, which enlightens everyone, was coming into the world" (John 1:9). Celtic Christian spiritual guide J. Philip Newell shares the essence of the Celtic attitude toward religious pluralism: "Typical of the Celtic mission was the practice of baptizing religious symbols and teachings from the pre-Christian nature mysticism. Columba, for instance, referred to Christ as his druid. Similarly many of the holy sites and groves were transformed into monastic bases for Christian mission. Christ was preached as the fulfilment of everything that was true, including the wisdom of the tradition that preceded Christianity in Celtic Britain."[5] God is generous in revealing divine wisdom and healing. Followers of the Way of Jesus are challenged to listen and learn from every wise spiritual, cultural, and intellectual movement, whether overtly religious or secular. In God's world, wherever truth or healing are present, God is its ultimate source.

These affirmations give birth to a green spirituality that honors the earth, and challenges us to become companions with, rather than destroyers of, our fragile ecosystem and its diverse flora and fauna.

---

5    J. Philip Newell, *The Book of Creation: An Introduction to Celtic Spirituality* (Mahweh, NY: Paulist Press, 1999), xx.

# CHAPTER THREE

## WITH BEAUTY ALL AROUND US WE LIVE:
## THE SPIRIT OF PROCESS THEOLOGY

In his inspiring reflection on humankind's intellectual and spiritual journey, *Adventures in Ideas,* the philosophical parent of process theology, Alfred North Whitehead, states that life begins with the dream of youth and finds completion in a harvest of tragic beauty. Beauty is at the heart of process theology. God leads the world adventure with the vision of truth, beauty, and goodness. Whitehead asserts that aim of the universe is toward the production of beauty, the blend of intensity, complexity, order, and dynamism that gives life to the universe and inspires the human spirit. Although process theology embraces the world of science, most especially quantum physics and evolutionary biology, process thought reenchants the world, transforming the apparently lifeless, valueless, and one-dimensional world of modern materialistic science, politics, and economics into the lively, relational, world of wonders, described by Maltbie Babcock's hymn:

> *This is my Father's world,*
> *and to my listening ears*
> *all nature sings, and round me rings*
> *the music of the spheres.*
> *This is my Father's world:*
> *I rest me in the thought*
> *of rocks and trees, of skies and seas;*
> *his hand the wonders wrought.*

While we rightly describe the Creative Wisdom of the Universe as both Mother and Father, process theology invites us to see the world as it really is, infinite in creativity, beauty, movement, and wonder. Amazement and appreciation are the only appropriate responses to the generous, creative, and wise hand of God, revealed in the birth of every moment, the soaring eagle, the intricacy of the immune system, the laughter of a child, and the fidelity of friendship. Process theology, along with Celtic spirituality, embodies the prayerfulness of Navajo spirit guides, whose world view also honors all creation as a manifestation of divine beauty:

> *In beauty I walk*
> *With beauty before me I walk*
> *With beauty behind me I walk*
> *With beauty above me I walk*
> *With beauty around me I walk.*

Theologian Karl Barth once described British religion as incurably Pelagian in its affirmation of humanity's essential goodness and agency in response to divine grace. While Barth meant this as a criticism, the British philosopher Whitehead and his Celtic Christian predecessors would have embraced Barth's critique as a positive affirmation of the interplay of divine call and human response in the quest for beauty, love, and justice. They would have recognized Augustine's insights into human sin and the priority of grace, affirmed by Barth, but would have reminded Barth that fallenness and passivity do not fully describe the human adventure. Flawed though we may be, we are wondrously made, the children of God's creative wisdom, able to imitate our creator in our agency, artistry, and adventure. God's grace calls for our own gracefulness. Divine creativity supports our own creativity.

Although it is unclear whether Whitehead or his first theological followers were schooled in Celtic spirituality, the spirit of process theology embraces the Celtic tradition's vision of a beautiful God whose wisdom gives birth to a lively, adventurous, free, and creative universe. The heart of process theology involves an array of lively and practical affirmations that shape our perspective, values, ethics, spiritual practices, and attitudes toward our planet and its creatures.

*First, process theology affirms that God is alive and moving through the universe in our souls and cells, in the evolution of planets and the birth of galaxies.* We live in a God-filled world in which divine creative wisdom moves through all creation. God is the reality in whom "we live and move and have our being" (Acts 17:28). God is our constant companion in every season life of life. As Psalm 139 proclaims:

> *If I ascend to heaven, you are there;*
> *if I make my bed in Sheol, you are there.*
> *If I take the wings of the morning*
> *and settle at the farthest limits of the sea,*
> *even there your hand shall lead me,*
> *and your right hand shall hold me fast.*
> *If I say, "Surely the darkness shall cover me,*
> *and the light around me become night,"*
> *even the darkness is not dark to you;*
> *the night is as bright as the day,*
> *for darkness is as light to you.* (Psalm 139:8-11)

When process theologians assert that God is with us, they truly mean it. With God as our companion "nothing [else] in all creation can separate us from the love of God" (Romans 8:39).

*Second, process theologians assert that God's creativity is best described as poetic, artistic, and ethical.* According Alfred North Whitehead, God is the poet of the universe, who guides the world by the vision of beauty of truth, goodness, and beauty. The divine artist paints a rainbow world of contrast, diversity, and creativity, working with the materials at hand, chance and freedom, to bring forth a work of beauty. God initiates and guides the moral arc of history. As nineteenth century American Unitarian minister Theodore Parker proclaimed, God bends the arc of history toward justice. This eventuates in the emergence of equality, diversity, and beauty. In each moment, God provides possibilities to maximize creativity, freedom, and intensity of experience, congruent with the overall well-being of our ourselves, our communities, our nation, and the world.

*Third, process theologians affirm that the world God creates is lively, creative, and innovative.* Creaturely freedom is real, even in relationship to God. Our choices matter to God and our planet's future. The world is a reflection of divine wisdom and creativity.

We live in a beautiful universe, grounded in God's evolving art-istry. God is not bound by the strait jacket of predestination and determinism. The world is incomplete and divine creativity is un-finished. A fully planned universe, in which nothing new happens to us or God, makes God's experience less interesting and lively than our own. Not trapped in past decisions, divine creativity brings forth a world in which freedom and chance are real. God is present in all things, but God's presence enhances rather than detracts from creaturely decision-making. God does not originate evil, plan the damnation of sinners in advance, or visualize in a timeless eternity the whole of our lives. At the very least, every creature has minimal creativity, emerging from its own vantage point on the universe. This ubiquitous creativity can bring froth anomalous cancer cells; it can also inspire in partnership with the Great Physician through experimental treatments, compassionate energy workers, and praying companions. Still, in the tumult of conflict, change, and evolution, God is "the ideal companion who transmutes what has been lost into a living fact within his own nature. He is the mirror that discloses to every creature its own greatness."[6] Delighting in human creativity, God constantly creates and responds in relationship to the world. We bring new things into God's experience and in return God provides new pathways for us to travel.

*Fourth, process theologians proclaim that creation in all its variety and levels of experience is alive and sings with the music of the spheres.* Value and experience are coextensive with reality. The human and non-human worlds burst forth in creativity. All things – described by Whitehead as "actual occasions," "actual entities," and "socie-ties of actual occasions" - are characterized by various degrees of experience, beginning with feelings of affirmation or aversion to their environment and expanding in higher creatures to experi-ences of love, innovation, imagination, intuition, and sacrifice. Schweitzer's vision of reverence for life is real: whatever exists from a chimpanzee, fetus, and bald eagle, to simpler organisms like jelly fish, earth worms, and fireflies, is a center of experience and crea-

---

6    Alfred North Whitehead, *Religion in the Making* (Cambridge: Cambridge University Press, 2011), 58.

tivity and deserves ethical consideration. While "life is robbery," as Whitehead notes, every creature makes a moral claim on us that we must consider, even when their lives are destroyed for what perceive to be a greater good. Insofar as we are able, reverence for life compels us to save the baby humans, but also to protect with equal commitment the baby right whales, of which there are less than 500 of these majestic creatures on the planet. Our reverence for life is inspired by God's love of the world. God notes the fall of the sparrow, the traumatized child following an incident of gun violence at her school or separation from her parents on America's borderlands, and the grief elephants experience at the loss of their mate.

*Fifth, process theology asserts that we are connected in a dynamic and intricate web of relationships.* Everything from planets to T-cells, is connected. The whole universe conspires, as Whitehead asserts, to create each occasion of experience and each moment of experience contributes to the world beyond itself. As I sit in my study, writing before sunrise, I am connected to the foreign policy crisis on the Korean peninsula, the grief of teenagers and parents in Parkland, Florida, the collapsing iceberg in the Arctic Circle, and my sleeping wife and Golden Doodle in the master bedroom. Our joys and sorrows are joined, in the spirit of I Corinthians 12:26. Our prayers make a difference. As medical research suggests, the energy of love in our prayers and meditative practices radiates across our neighborhoods and the planet without regard to distances in space and time.

*Sixth, process theologians rejoice in the reality that God's love is both creative and responsive.* God is the fellow sufferer who understands and the companioning celebrant who rejoices. God is the inspiration of novelty and creativity in the universe, inspiring each moment of experience with a vision of what it can be. What that moment of experience becomes shapes God's experience and serves as the inspiration for God's future involvement in the world. As the book of Jonah poetically asserts, God calls Nineveh initially through a vision of destruction, which will occur if the people maintain their current course of action. Then, "God changes God's mind" in response to the Ninevite's repentance. God feels their fear and desire to change. God feels the grief of a parent whose child is gunned down on an urban street corner. God also experiences the elation of child scoring a goal in soccer, a whale breaching off Cape Cod, and a dog racing on the beach.

These descriptions are intended to be poetic and evocative rather than technical. Sadly, Whitehead's technical language and the desire among some process theologians to be in synch with the minutia of Whitehead's cosmology has made process theology inaccessible and problematic even to educated readers. Process theology's life transforming vision educates the intellect, but just as importantly inspires the heart, enlivens the spirit, and energizes our relationships. As theologian Patricia Adams Farmer states, process theology awakens us to a beautiful God and the grandeur of our own spirits as God's companions in a beautiful world. With Celtic spiritual guides and Navajo sages, process theology inspires a re-enchanted world, green spirituality and commitment to nurturing our planet in all its wondrous beauty. In reclaiming indigenous and early Christian wisdom, we find guidance for facing today's political and environmental crises.

> *Through the returning seasons, may I walk.*
> *On the trail marked with pollen may I walk.*
> *With dew about my feet, may I walk.*
> *With beauty before me may I walk.*
> *With beauty behind me may I walk.*
> *With beauty below me may I walk.*
> *With beauty above me may I walk.*
> *With beauty all around me may I walk.*
> *In old age wandering on a trail of beauty, lively,*
> *may I walk.*
> *In old age wandering on a trail of beauty, living again, may I walk.*
> *My words will be beautiful.*[7]

7    https://talking-feather.com/home/walk-in-beauty-prayer-from-navajo-blessing/

# CHAPTER FOUR

## THIN PLACES EVERYWHERE

Process theology and Celtic Christianity describe a lively, green, and God-filled universe. The heavens declare the glory of God and so does our immune system. The divine imprint is revealed in all creation, human and non-human alike. English poet and priest Gerard Manley Hopkins sees the world as the canvas for divine artistry: "the world is charged with the grandeur of God." God's Spirit hovers over all creation and bursts forth within all creation. Despite our desecration of God's world, in all creatures "there lives the dearest freshness deep down things."[8] Those who train their ears can, with the hymn writer Maltbie Babcock, "hear God's voice everywhere." As poet Kenneth White notes, "I have grown chrysanthemums on the dung of God."[9]

The biblical tradition chronicles the adventures of the patriarch Jacob, who falls asleep one night, only to dream of a ladder of angels mounting from earth to heaven and then back again. Upon waking, Jacob stammers, "Surely the LORD is in this place—and I did not know it!... How awesome is this place! This is none other than the house of God, and this is the gate of heaven" (Genesis 28:16-17). Later, the patriarch encounters a mysterious visitor, with whom he wrestles all night long, and from whom he receives a divine blessing (Genesis 32:22-32). Two thousand years later, Jesus' disciples are overwhelmed when their teacher is bathed in divine light along with Elijah and Moses. These dramatic encounters with the Holy reveal the epiphanic nature of reality, described centuries later by William Blake, "If the doors of perception were cleansed, everything would appear to man as it is, infinite."

---

8    Gerard Manley Hopkins, "God's Grandeur."
9    Quoted in J. Philip Newell, *The Book of Creation: An Introduction to Cetlic Spirituality* (Mahweh, NJ: Paulist Press, 1999), 37.

Beth-el was surely a "thin place," where heaven and earth burst forth in God's glory and Jacob's life was forever changed. Earth angels can be found anywhere. Divine radiance revealed heaven on the mountain top and opened the disciples to Jesus' true identity as God's beloved Savior. God's radiance opens our eyes and reveals our own true identity as loved by God.

Process theology asserts that God is present in the emergence of each moment of experience in terms of guidance, possibility, and energy. God's aim at beauty of experience, appropriate to each moment and every environment, gives life and direction to all things. Moreover, every occasion deep down reveals God's vision to us. Every face reflects something of divinity. In similar fashion, Celtic Christianity proclaimed the importance of "thin places," environments transparent to divinity, where heaven and earth meet to inspire, guide, and transform our lives. Following the wisdom of the indigenous druidic spirituality, Celtic Christians discerned God's presence in groves of trees, babbling brooks, rock formations, and rocky islands. Certain sites such as Stonehenge, Avebury, Glastonbury, Landisfarne, and Iona, were identified as places where divinity most especially reveals itself. Pilgrims still experience vortices of revelation in places like Sedona, Mecca, Jerusalem, and the Ganges River. Charged with divine wisdom and energy, these sacred spaces awaken our spirits and point us to the deeper realities of the universe. They proclaim to the pilgrim, "You are standing on holy ground, with a myriad of angels all around."

A number of years ago, while teaching a course on Jesus' healing ministry at Ghost Ranch in Northern New Mexico, I found myself drawn to a chimney rock, or hoodoo, a tall, thin rock formation jutting out from earth. As I walked toward the hoodoo each morning at sunrise, I felt kinship with the First American spiritual guides who saw these rock formations as holy spots, revealing divine wisdom. I experienced the artistry of Georgia O'Keefe, who lived on the other side of the chimney rock and claimed my own identity as an artist of the spirit, bringing forth the beauty and grandeur of creation in my own novel fashion. The wildness of the USA southwest reminds the pilgrim of the wildness of the Scottish and Irish coast.

The universe, described by Celtic Christian spirit guides and process theologians is translucent to divinity. Process theology echoes the nascent Celtic insight that God is both omnipresent and omni-active. The wise creativity of God is the deepest reality of all things. Despite our turning from God's way, God still moves through all creation, turning the world from darkness to light, and giving birth to beauty where humans see only ugliness. The ever-present God, however, is not a homogenous, undifferentiated force, indifferent to beauty and goodness. Present in all things, God can choose to be more present in some places and persons than others. Some places are truly gateways to heaven. Some times are the right moment for personal and cultural transformation. Some persons are transparent to divine healing and revelatory power. God brings forth thin places, Kairos moments, and wise women and men. God is incarnate everywhere and this global incarnation gave birth to God's glorious incarnation in a Bethlehem stable.

At the heart of Celtic spirituality is the concept of "*anamcara*," the friend of the soul, the person in whose face I see the face of God and my true identity. Columba once asserted that Christ is our druid, that is, our teacher and healer. Christ is also our *anamcara,* the friend of our souls, who reveals to us our own divinity, and gives us the vision to see beyond the surface and discover God's image often disguised by our own fears and fallibility. In the spirit of Whitehead, Christ is the mirror who reveals to us our greatness, even when we feel most fallible and unworthy.

In her "thin" encounter with the angel Gabriel, Mary, the mother of Jesus, becomes the "theotokos," the mother of God, incarnate in our world. Whether in the conception of Jesus or the birth of a humpbacked whale, the world lives by the incarnation of God, as Whitehead asserts, and this life-giving incarnation can be found in Jesus of Nazareth, his mother Mary, Magi from the East, refugees seeking asylum, and every mother's child. It can be found in us! Incarnation is grace, that saves the lost, welcomes the pilgrim, and heals the broken. Embracing incarnation as global gives us inspiration and energy to embrace the outcast, protest injustice, pray for our benighted leaders, and claim our vocation as God's companions in healing the earth.

## CHAPTER FIVE

### CREATION SINGS

The Celtic sages describe our world as an enchanted reality. Process theologians invite digitized twenty-first century seekers to embrace the re-enchantment of nature. Modern humankind has abandoned the garden of delight in which all nature sings with the music of the spheres. We have made our earth a garbage dump, focusing on consumption rather than contemplation and acquisition rather than appreciation. Earth is in the balance, as permafrost melts releasing toxic gases such as mercury into the atmosphere, rising temperatures threaten coastal populations, politicians release wilderness lands for oil drilling, and species habitats are destroyed. The chant, "Drill, baby, drill," in all its sexualized objectification, has replaced "let everything that breathes, praise God" in their economic and religious values. With destruction all around, we need a new transformation of the spirit that comes from an alternative way of looking at the world. We need to reimagine our planet to value beauty as much as profit, future generations as much as momentary consumption, and planetary well-being as much as national security.

The early Christian affirmation, "wherever truth is present, God is its source," means that we can affirm the scientific adventure in life-supporting ways. We need to utilize new technologies and scientific discoveries in ways that heal, rather than harm the earth. This is the meaning of "re-enchantment," the process of embracing human achievement in the context of affirming the value of non-human life and the planet as whole apart from human interests.

Process theology and Celtic spirituality affirm the biblical vision of a God-filled universe, transparent to God and valued in God's sight. We live in a world of praise, as Psalm 148 proclaims, in which our prayers echo the prayers of all creation:

*Praise God, sun and moon;*
*praise God, all you shining stars!*
*Praise God, you highest heavens,*
*and you waters above the heavens!*
*Let them praise the name of the LORD....*

*Praise the LORD from the earth,*
*you sea monsters and all deeps,*
*fire and hail, snow and frost,*
*stormy wind fulfilling his command!*

*Mountains and all hills,*
*fruit trees and all cedars!*
*Wild animals and all cattle,*
*creeping things and flying birds!*

*Kings of the earth and all peoples,*
*princes and all rulers of the earth!*
*Young men and women alike,*
*old and young together!*

Though I cited this Psalm earlier, the crises of our time require the repetition of life-affirming chants and mantras to change our minds and transform our behaviors. Humankind is rooted in a world of beauty and delight. A living universe in which the heavens declare the glory of God along with imaginative artists, gliding swans, and the cells of our bodies. Celtic spirituality and process theology affirm the university of experience. While there are different levels of experience, all creatures, human, non-human, plant, and vegetable, are responsive to their environments. All creatures are able to praise as they turn Godward in attention. An ever-present, ever-active God undergirds and permeates every aspect of creation, without exception.

Today, the sciences are inviting us to imaginatively reenchant the non-human world in the healing interplay of head, heart, and hands. Observation as well as scientific study tell us that the world within and the world beyond is chockfull of vibrancy and experience. Studies of crows indicate that they can problem solve with the same sophistication as a human toddler, and that they can defer gratification for up to five minutes to achieve a greater goal, something few humans of any age are able to achieve! The Japanese researcher Masuru Emoto conjectures, based on photographic images, that water crystals can be influenced by positive and negative human emotions. Biologist George David Haskell believes that trees "speak constantly, even if quietly, communicating above- and underground using sound, scents, signals, and vibes. They're *naturally networking,* connected with everything that exists, including you." In her research on underground fungal networks, ecologist Susan Simard invites us "to change the way you think about forests. You see, underground there is this other world, a world of infinite biological pathways that connect trees and allow them to communicate and allow the forest to behave as though it's a single organism. It might remind you of a sort of intelligence."[10]

In contrast to the modern humankind's devaluing and desensitizing of the non-human world, indigenous peoples and Celtic Christians see the world as alive. Trees and groves have spirits. Birds communicate with us. Sometimes they simply sing for the pure joy of it, as process philosopher Charles Hartshorne avers. Dolphins and whales – dare we say, mermaids – help sailors in distress. Celtic spiritual guide Ninian's confession proclaims that the first goal of religious study is "to perceive the eternal word of God, reflected in every plant and insect, in every bird and animal, man and woman."[11]

By focusing solely on humankind and otherworldly salvation, "orthodox" Christians promote devastation of the non-human world. They emphasize dominion in terms of self-interest rather than stewardship. A senseless earth has no value apart from human goals, seen in terms of construction, profit, and power. A senseless earth is the front porch to eternity rather than God's beautiful world. Scripture was seen as the proof text for profiteering and objectification of the non-human world. In the words of

---

10    https://qz.com/1116991/a-biologist-believes-that-trees-speak-a-language-we-can-learn/
11    Kenneth McIntosh, *Water from an Ancient Well: Celtic Spirituality for Modern Life* (Vestal, NY: Anamchara Books, 2014), 129.

Joni Mitchell, senseless faith, joined with acquisitive economics, "paved paradise and put up a parking lot."

Our vision of the world guides our ethics and our spirituality. In the context of global climate change, species extinction, and the wilderness destruction, we need now more than ever creative earth-affirming ethics, that embrace the well-being of the non-human world in all its wondrous variety. Process theology and Celtic spirituality expand the circle of ethics to include our relationships with the world of land animals, birds, sea creatures, and the earth itself. While levels of experience, complexity, and creativity vary among creatures, whatever has experience deserves ethical consideration, apart from its impact on humankind in terms of profit, loss, and appreciation. Values in the non-human world and between humans and non-humans may be at cross purposes and sacrifices need to be made. Some forms of destruction are inevitable. But, the destruction of woodlands and killing of non-human creatures requires significant ethical justification. Our survival and life-style benefits must outweigh the pain and death we inflict on the non-human world.

The green spirituality affirmed in process theology and Celtic wisdom sees the promotion of life in its diversity as the primary ecological challenge of our time. Being pro-life takes us far beyond the ethical challenges of abortion to our attitudes toward war, incarceration, and species survival. We are ethically challenged to save both baby humans and baby whales, whenever possible. The survival of the less than 500 right whales I mentioned earlier, many of whom gather on bay near my home on Cape Cod matters because of their experience of pain and joy. It also matters because the richness of creation and God's own richness of experience is diminished with the extinction of any species. The artist of the universe paints with a broad and diverse palette and rejoices in the partnership of divine and creaturely creativity.

The universality of experience, affirmed in process theology and Celtic spirituality, is evident in the Celtic recognition of groves of trees and rock formations as thin and holy places, translucent to divinity. The green spirituality engendered by process theology and its Celtic companions inspires appreciative spiritual and ethical practices. While I spend an hour each day in quiet meditation, I also pray each day with my eyes open, bathing my senses in beauty as I rise and look at the stars upon awakening each morning, as I pause to watch a bird in flight, gaze at leaves stirred by a gentle breeze. On my morning walk at the beach near my home, I not only pray for friends, political leaders, and the world, I also gaze with gratitude at the rolling waves and expansive Nantucket Sound. Prior to turning in each night, I go out on patio and gaze at the heavens, often considering the amazing reality that I share the same wonder with the Psalmist who proclaimed "the heavens are telling the glory of God and the firmament proclaims his handiwork" (Psalm 19:1). Radical amazement is the only fitting response to the wonders of the universe, the luminous flight of a fire fly on a summer night, the halting steps of a toddler, the intricacy of a human cell, my Golden Doodle bounding across the yard to greet me, or the stars that inspire us on a clear winter's eve. From radical amazement comes equally radical commitment to speaking for our voiceless planet and living simply so that our non-human and human companions can simply live.

# CHAPTER SIX

## DAILY BLESSINGS

Jewish wisdom proclaims that when you save one soul you save the world. According to the Jewish mystics, the world will not be healed until every lost sheep is found and every lost child returns home to loving arms. Each moment is a moment of salvation, as twelve step groups speak of sober living one day at a time. The importance of living prayerfully moment by moment is at the heart of process theology and Celtic spirituality. Process theology asserts that every moment of experience is guided by God's vision. According to Whitehead, "Every event on its finer side introduces God into the world…the power by which God sustains the world is the power of himself as the ideal …The world lives by the incarnation of God in itself."[12] God seeks the best possibility for us in every moment, given our past history and personal and social context. Time and space alike reveal divinity. Each moment is a theophany, a revealing of God's vision, and every moment can become an epiphany when we dedicate ourselves to discerning God's will in the responsibilities and demands of daily life.

The Celts believed that daily life was a crucible within which we live out our faith. Every moment calls us to prayerful God-awareness. Each moment leans toward an open future, determined by the interplay of God's call, our response, the decisions of those around us. Upon waking, we can open our lives to the energy of love, embodied in divine providence, sufficient for every need, or we can place self-interest and profit ahead of our responsibilities to God's good creation. We can embrace the uncertain future knowing that God is our companion, providing us with everything we need to respond to life's challenges or we can mold the world to suit our prerogatives regardless of the cost to future generations of human and non-humans. The Celts challenge us to seek the

---

12    Alfred North Whitehead, *Religion in the Making*, 149.

first path, the way of humble affirmation of divine creativity and creaturely beauty, as we open our eyes each morning.

*I arise today*
*With the might of heaven:*
*The rays of the sun,*
*The beams of the moon,*
*The glory of fire,*
*The speed of wind,*
*The depth of sea,*
*The stability of earth,*
*The hardness of rock.* [13]

As we leave our homes each morning, heading to work, school, church, or exercise, we can depart with a spirit of adventure. In the face of the unfolding day, we can surround ourselves in prayers for guidance and wisdom:

*I on thy path, O God.*
*Thou God in my steps.*
*Bless me, O God*
*The earth beneath my foot,*
*Bless me, O God,*
*The path whereon I go.* [14]

Alfred North Whitehead asserted that the world lives by God's moment-by-moment vision and that every action either adds or subtracts from God's presence in the world. Our daily lives, down to the smallest task, reflect our response to divine guidance and shape our own and the world's future. Nothing is unimportant and nothing is all-important. God is equally present in the secular as in the sacred; in fact, we can praise God in our work as well as in our worship, in our plans as well as our prayers, and in our calendars as well as our contemplation. Our livelihoods are intended to give glory to God and support the well-being of our communities. A God-inspired life joins work and prayer, and becomes itself a prayer

---

13   Robert Van de Weyer, *Celtic Fire,* 79.
14   Esther de Waal, *Every Earthly Blessing,* (Harrisburg, PA: Moorehouse, 1999), p. 9.

in our attentiveness to God's inspiration emerging in our own experience and in the actions of those around us. Inspired by God's presence in our daily tasks, we can, with French mystic Therese of Lisieux, do ordinary things with great love, knowing that our approach to work can help or hurt those around us and contribute or detract from our own spiritual growth. We may not be dairy farmers but we can, with the Celtic earth mother St. Brigid, see God as the inspiration of our daily task, doing something beautiful for God in every endeavor.

> *Come, Mary, and milk my cow,*
> *Come, Bride, and encompass her,*
> *Come, Columba the benign*
> *And twine thine arm around my cow.*
> *Come, Mary Virgin, to my cow,*
> *Come, great Bride, the beauteous,*
> *Come, thou milk maid of Jesus Christ,*
> *And place thine arms beneath my cow.* [15]

Then, at day's end, we give thanks for God's blessings and companionship in the adventures of each day, trusting that as we sleep we rest in divine care.

> *God bless to me this day,*
> *God bless to me this night;*
> *Bless, O Bless, Thou God of grace,*
> *Each day and hour of my life;*
> *Bless, O Bless, Thou God of grace,*
> *Each day and hour of my life.*
> *God bless the pathway on which I go,*
> *God bless the earth that is beneath my sole;*
> *Bless, O God, and give to me Thy love,*
> *O God of Gods, bless my rest and my repose;*
> *Bless, O God, and give to me Thy love,*
> *And bless, O God of gods, my repose.* [16]

---

15    de Waal, *Every Earthly Blessing*, p. 5.
16    de Waal, *The Celtic Way of Prayer*, p. 90.

The ladder of angels rises, as the patriarch Jacob discovers, right where we are. Holiness is found in the here and now. As Jesus called his first followers on the seashore, God beckons us to follow him right where we are. The spiritual journey moves from Jacob's exclamation, "God was in this place – and I did not know it!" to our affirmation "God is in this place – and I awaken to God's vision." With physician, missionary, organist, and biblical scholar Albert Schweitzer, whose walk with God inspired his reverence for all creation, we can affirm that God's calls and, in the walking, we find our way:

> He comes to us as One unknown, without a name, as of old, by the lakeside. He came to those men who knew Him not. He speaks to us the same words: "Follow thou me!" and sets us to the tasks which He has to fulfill for our time. He commands. And to those who obey Him, whether they be wise or simple, He will reveal himself in the toils, the conflicts, the sufferings which they shall pass through in His fellowship, and, as an ineffable mystery, they shall learn in their own experience Who He is.[17]

In the relational world, visualized by process theology and Celtic spirituality, our lives are not our own. We are the children of our families, institutions, cultures, and nations. What we do radiates beyond ourselves, shaping the future of our companions and communities. Each apparently unique and individual moment of creation stretches out into infinity in both time and space. Our lives are, accordingly, political and ethical in nature. What we do and how do it can harm or heal, create or destroy, embrace or alienate. The simple moments of life – a Facebook post, conversation with the checkout person at the store, welcome to a person of another faith, nationality, or ethnicity – quietly but persistently transform the world. Our consumption, property usage, and financial decision-making are never merely individual matters. The interdependence of life compels us to hold rights and responsibilities in creative tension. Freedom is never, nor should it ever be, absolute. Our freedom is intended to encourage our well-being,

---

17    Albert Schwietzer, *Albert Schweitzer: The Essential Writings* (Maryknoll, NY: Orbis Books, 2005, 41.

the well-being of those around us, and the well-being of the planet in the intricate and interdependent ecology of life.

Whitehead asserts that "religion is world loyalty."[18]  Our daily lives flow into our responsibilities as national and planetary citizens. Aligning ourselves with God's universal aim at beauty requires that we constantly ask ourselves questions such as: Will this behavior add or subtract from the beauty of life?  Do my actions, including my consumption and political involvement, promote the best interests of the least acknowledge in my community and nation? We cannot be uninvolved bystanders when seas are rising, politicians threaten nuclear war, children are killed in classrooms, and young adults are threatened with deportation from the only country they've ever known.  In turning to God's call to move from individualism to interdependence, our actions tip the scale from death to life for our children and children's children. In following God's vision of beauty and compassion, we affirm a politics and ethics of love and beauty that embraces creation in all its wondrous, and sometimes conflicting, diversity.

---

18   Alfred North Whitehead, *Religion in the Making*, 59.

# Chapter Seven

One of my mentors, process theologian David Ray Griffin, once asserted that "God wants us to enjoy; God wants us all to enjoy." God's aim at beauty and intensity of experience embraces the whole human race, without exception. God's vision of truth, beauty, and goodness inspires the "moral arc of history," bending it toward justice. Injustice, poverty, marginalization, and oppression – and all the "isms" of our world – stunt the imagination, close the heart, and numb the spirits of oppressor and oppressed and perpetrator and victim. God's vision of our personal and corporate well-being is moment by moment, and each moment contributes to God's vision for the long haul. God's vision is for this place and time, but it also promotes the positive impact of each moment on our broader relational and social context. We seek justice so that our spirits may soar, the child in all of us laugh and play, and the artist in each of us burst forth in creative adventure. Injustice not only deadens the human spirit, but tarnishes God's own experience and limits God's work in the world.

Although Celtic Christianity did not fashion a specific social ethic, the Celtic sages sought to be attuned to the way of Jesus and Jesus' own mission to bring abundant life to all creation. The Spirit of God, Jesus asserted, leans toward hospitality, healing, and justice. In his own vision statement, taken from the social prophet Isaiah, Jesus proclaimed:

> *The Spirit of the Lord is upon me,*
> *because he has anointed me*
> *to bring good news to the poor.*
> *He has sent me to proclaim release to the captives*
> *and recovery of sight to the blind,*
> *to let the oppressed go free,*
> *to proclaim the year of the Lord's favor.* (Luke 4:18-19)

The year of God's favor, God's jubilee year, when God's Shalom guides human communities, is the polestar which guides our social and political involvement. Both process theology and Celtic spirituality believe that God not only desires our partnership, but needs us to be companions in healing the world. We are the ones who open the spiritual and ethical floodgates to "let justice roll down like waters, and righteousness like an ever-flowing stream" (Amos 5:24).

Justice seeking and earth care is serious business, but the gravity of our work is also lightened by the levity of divine grace. Justice is about celebration and joy, creativity and exploration, possibility and adventure, and value and wonder, not just for the few but for all. No one captures the playful process of justice seeking than the Celtic spiritual guide Brigid:

> *I should like a lake of finest ale*
> *For the king of kings.*
> *I should like a table of the choicest food*
> *For the family of heaven.*
> *Let the ale be made from the fruits of the earth*
> *And the food be forgiving love.*
> *I should welcome the poor to my feast,*
> *For they are God's children.*
> *I should welcome the sick to my feast,*
> *For they are God's joy.*
> *Let the poor sit with Jesus at the highest place.*
> *And the sick dance with the angels.*
> *God bless the poor,*
> *God bless the sick,*
> *And bless our human race*
> *God bless our food,*
> *God bless our drink,*
> *All homes, O God, embrace.*[19]

Like Mary's Magnificat, which portrays God feeding the hungry, and sending the rich away empty-handed, Brigid's feast turns upside down our society's value system, giving a preferential option

19   de Weyer, *Celtic Fire*, p. 20-22

to the poor and sick. The realm of God, Brigid says, is a glorious banquet, given for Jesus, with everyone invited regardless of race, ethnicity, class, sexuality, or economics. Everything is eucharistic, healing souls, cells, and societies.

The foundation for justice seeking and social concern is the intricate and dynamic interdependence of life. Process theology and Celtic spirituality visualize the world as a wondrous interdependent organism. Whatever we do privately, whether in our spiritual lives or interpersonal encounters, goes forth into the broader world. Social action changes things, and so does prayer. We are not self-made, nor are we isolated individuals. No woman is an island, nor is any nation. In the dynamic interdependence of life, our actions radiate across the planet, creating environments of hope or hovels of despair.

On Valentine's Day 2018, seventeen students and teachers were killed in a mass shooting at a Florida high school. Though the shootings took place over 1,300 miles from my home on Cape Cod, as a grandparent of two young boys, my heart was broken as I viewed the scene of anxious parents waiting in the school parking lot, teenagers running from the school grounds to meet their parents, and later parents, friends, and relatives sobbing when their worst nightmare came to pass. What happens in Florida shapes my quality in life. Later that Valentine's Day, I was extra vigilant as I picked up my grandchildren from school, grateful that there were no "copy cats." Decisions in Tallahassee, Florida, and Washington DC, determine whether school children live or die in terms of gun safety, health insurance, environmental pollution, and diet. Phone calls to political leaders can shift the balance from death to life for undocumented workers, Syrian refugees, inner city children, or impoverished senior citizens. We are all part of the dynamic body of Christ in which "If one member suffers, all suffer together with it; if one member is honored, all rejoice together with it" (I Corinthians 12:26).

Brigid saw Christian ethics and social responsibility in terms of a "lake of ale" where all receive the fullness of joy and the sounds of the streets are filled with laughter. Celebration, exploration, fulfillment, and wholeness is what justice-seeking is all about, to the Celtic saint. God is throwing a party – the creation of a beautiful universe – and wants everyone to share God's joy. Whitehead describes the joyful arc of the universe in terms of divine artistry: "God is the poet of the world, with tender patience leading it by his vision of truth, beauty, and goodness."[20]

In an interdependent world, we matter to one another and we matter to God. God is the fellow sufferer who understands, the ultimate recipient of the tears and sorrow of the world. God is also the joyful celebrant who inspires moments of wonder and delight. With Mother Teresa of Calcutta, our calling is simply to do something beautiful for God by adding to the beauty of experience of those around us. That is the ultimate ethical issue, loving the Creator by nurturing beauty of experience among God's beloved creatures. In our day to day interpersonal and broad spectrum political perspectives, the key question is: "Do we want to give God beauty or ugliness by our actions in our relationships, family life, community involvement, and political decision-making?"

In an interdependent world, none of us is an "innocent bystander." There is nowhere to hide in terms of the impact of our actions on the world around us and the impact of the world in shaping our experience and expanding or limiting our possibilities.

Process interpersonal and social ethics challenge us to choose life by promoting life giving experiences. As I stated earlier, value is co-extensive with reality. Celtic poets rejoiced in the joy felt by a singing bird or stag racing across an open field. Process theologians speak of each creature as a unique center of experience, responding uniquely to its environment. Ethics is grounded in empathy, the recognition that others, including our enemies and the non-human world, feel joy or sorrow. Following God's vision, we seek an ethics of personal stature that enables us to experience the joys and sorrows of a woman who identifies herself as "me, too" in terms of sexual harassment, an African American teen who asserts that "black lives matter," a growing fetus whose sensitivity to his environment increases with each month in the womb, and a young mother who must make a difficult decision regarding the future of

---

20    Alfred North Whitehead, *Process and Reality: Corrected Edition* (New York: Free Press, 1979), 346.

that same fetus. The quest for beauty of experience is grounded in our ability to acknowledge the feelings, the experiences, the value of the other, and take these feelings into our own lives. Such empathy may trouble us but it is also the source of peace, the experience of the widening of the spirit to embrace the joy of pain of others.

Ethics on the personal and political realm is ultimately about "growing in wisdom and stature," promoting beauty of experience, and openness to the values of others in shaping our experiences of the world. Process theologian Bernard Loomer affirms an ethics of personal stature, prerequisite for a truly holistic social ethic:

> *By size I mean the stature of a person's soul,*
> *the range and depth of his love, his capacity for relationships.*
> *I mean the volume of life you can take into your*
> *being and still maintain your integrity and*
> *individuality, the intensity and variety of*
> *outlook you can entertain in the unity of*
> *your being without feeling defensive or insecure.*
> *I mean the strength of your spirit to encourage others to become freer*
> *in the development of their diversity and uniqueness.*[21]

For both Celtic Christians and process theologians, social ethics takes us beyond our own well-being and our own particular ideology to support the well-being of larger and larger communities of care. No one can be left behind or disenfranchised. Left and right, poor and wealthy, socialist and capitalist, belong in the circle of conversation and political involvement. As A.J. Muste noted, "There is no way to peace. Peace is the way." A lively creation requires giving non-humans ethical consideration. It also requires all sides of the abortion debate to recognize the value of both women and fetuses as worthy of consideration. We do not need to devalue fetal existence to affirm the value, creativity, and freedom of women. While there are unique qualities of human life and level of experience that need to be respected and considered in every ethical decision, we must also recognize that crows, dolphins, whales, chimps, and dogs have more complex experiences than

---

21 Bernard Loomer, "S-I-Z-E is the Measure," Harry James Cargas and Bernard Lee, *Religious Experience and Process Theology,* 70.

fetuses and even neonates. Right whales and newborn children are both cherished by God.

In the interdependent world, affirmed by both process theology and Celtic spirituality, we need to practice economics as if people mattered. We also need to judge the positive benefits of economic growth in terms of its impact on the non-human world. While we can legitimately wrestle with ethical issues regarding species preservation in relationship to job creation and economic gain, the loss of any species is felt by God and diminishes the quality of divine experience, such that species preservation may outweigh economic growth. The scale tips more in favor of species survival when we recognize that the majority of profit goes to those who are already wealthy and not to workers and struggling communities.

Ultimately, social ethics – the ethics of interdependence – is about Brigid's "lake of ale." God wants all of us to enjoy, and while we may give preference to our species, we must also invite the birds of the air, leaping dolphins, pangolins, monarch butterflies and honey bees, hammerhead sharks, spotted owls, and right whales to join us in God's realm of Shalom where gratitude, grace, and glee reign supreme.

# Chapter Eight

## Christ to Guide Me

The world cries out for a healing of purpose. We are in crisis and we need to recalibrate our Spiritual GPS from rugged individualism to creative freedom-affirming community, from consumerism to simplicity of spirit, from nation-first to world loyalty, from pride of class and race to graceful interdependence, from God-forsaken self-interest to planetary healing. We need the guidance of healthy and earth-affirming theological visions and spiritual practices. Once again, we need to meditate on the Prayer of St. Patrick as an antidote to anxiety and a guide through this present chaos:

> *I arise today Through God's strength to pilot me;*
> *God's might to uphold me, God's wisdom to guide me,*
> *God's eye to look before me, God's ear to hear me,*
> *God's word to speak for me, God's hand to guard me,*
> *God's way to lie before me, God's shield to protect me,*
> *God's hosts to save me Near and far.*
> *Christ with me, Christ before me, Christ behind me,*
> *Christ in me, Christ beneath me, Christ above me,*
> *Christ on my right, Christ on my left,*
> *Christ when I lie down, Christ when I sit down,*
> *Christ in the heart of everyone who thinks of me,*
> *Christ in the mouth of everyone who speaks of me,*
> *Christ in the eye that sees me,*
> *Christ in the ear that hears me.*

We need God's guidance in our personal lives and in our social, institutional, and religious context. Spiritual leaders and congregations face unprecedented cultural and religious shifts that threaten the very survival of institutional religion. We live in a dynamic, interdependent, rapidly changing world of pluralism and relativism in which doctrine has been supplanted by experience and authority has shifted from hierarchy and institution to individuality. Christianity, and the other major religions, must, as John Shelby Spong, asserts, change or die.

In times of rapid transformation, we need more rather than less theological reflection. But, our theological visions must be humble, evolving, relational, and life-affirming. They must honor personal and communal experience as a source of theological insight and affirm the mystical potential of everyone.

Patrick's prayer joins the universal and the personal. God's truth is global: wherever truth and healing are found, God is its source. Persons of faith, and particularly Christians, Jews, and Muslims, need not fear pluralism. God is the ultimate source of variety and diversity, whether it be in the world of plants, animals, races, or religions. In the spirit of the Celtic Christian tradition, Christianity flourishes when it honors and learns from other religious traditions and practices as well as literature, science, medicine, and faithful agnosticism. Celtic spiritual guide Columba affirmed "Christ is my druid" and his companions in the faith embraced the earth-based religions of the British Isles with their sacred spaces and times. In their affirmation of God's universal revelation, process theology and Celtic spirituality welcome the insights of other faith traditions.

Today, many people practice hybrid spiritualities in combining the wisdom of various religious traditions in their spiritual practices. In today's inter-spiritual world, ministers contemplate scripture and practice yoga, choir members go to bible studies and Zen Buddhist retreats, and congregants are inspired by Taize Christian chants and Sufi dances. We can affirm the wisdom of Jesus, from the perspective of our denominational, personal, and theological affirmations, while embracing God's wisdom broadcast in all creation.

A Celtic-process approach to evangelism honors others' spiritual experience while sharing the good news of Jesus. We trust spiritual transformation to God as we do our part in providing intellectual, spiritual, relational, and economic nourishment to others. We have good news to tell, and it is the news that God is with us, moving in our lives, embracing our pain and celebrating our success. We have the good news that Christ is inspiring us and divine wisdom and creativity is always making a way when perceive no way forward. We can confidently share the amazing grace of God's presence, "before, behind, beneath, above, on the left and on the right, within me and beyond me." We can affirm that God blesses me in every encounter and that our faith in Christ challenges us to bless one another.

In this spirit, our faith opens us to the future and our companions everyone, seeking wholeness and transformation. Our faith inspires adventure, inclusion, and evolution. As Whitehead affirms:

*Religion is the vision of something which stands beyond,*
*behind, and within the passing flux of immediate things;*
*something which is real, and yet waiting to be realized;*
*something which is a remote possibility,*
*and yet the greatest of present facts;*
*something that gives meaning to all that passes*
*and yet eludes apprehension;*
*something whose possession is the final good*
*and yet is beyond all reach;*
*something which is the ultimate ideal, and the hopeless quest.*[22]

The horizon of faith is ever-receding and never fully realized, and this is good news. For though we may never find a final resting place in our quest for planetary healing, we are never alone, "God is the fellow sufferer who understands" and the loving companion who empathizes and heals.[23] Recognizing God's intimate guidance, we can pray with the Celtic hymn, "Be Thou My Vision" and then pay attention to divine inspiration sufficient for every challenge:

*Be Thou my Vision, O God of my heart;*
*Naught be all else to me, save that Thou art.*
*Thou my best Thought, by day or by night,*
*Waking or sleeping, Thy presence my light.*
*Be Thou my Wisdom, and Thou my true Word;*
*I ever with Thee and Thou with me, Lord;*

---

22 Alfred North Whitehead, *Science and the Modern World* (New York: Free Press) , 191-192)

23 Alfred North Whitehead, *Process and Reality: Corrected Edition*, 351.

*Thou my great Father, I Thy true son;*
*Thou in me dwelling, and I with Thee one.*[24]

In times of danger and change, or as they embarked on pilgrimages, Celtic adventurers drew a circle around themselves in the direction of the sunrise, reminding them that God encircled their every step. In times of peril, they knew that they could call upon God and God would provide a way through the wilderness. We need to draw these same circles around ourselves and our beloved institutions. The future of the planet and our future remains in doubt; the winds of change and the pounding waves buffet our beloved institutions. Still, the dynamic life-affirming vision of God's creative-responsive love gives us confidence that we will have the resources to claim our role as God's companions in healing the earth. "Through many danger, toil, and snare," divine wisdom will have the final word and that word is love, or as Whitehead proclaims, "At the heart of the nature of things, there are always the dream of youth and the harvest of tragedy. The Adventure of the Universe starts with the dream and reaps tragic beauty. This is the secret of the union of Zest with Peace – that the suffering attains is end in a Harmony of Harmonies. The immediate experience of this Final Fact, with its union of Youth and Tragedy, is the sense of Peace. In this way the world receives its persuasion towards such possibilities as are possible for its diverse individual occasions."[25]   Thanks be to the Beautiful and Loving God whose vision challenges us to heal the earth.

---

24 You may choose to use "Parent" or "child" in the second verse in recognition of the egalitarian and inclusive spirituality of Celtic Christianity.
25 Alfred North Whitehead, *Adventures of Ideas* (New York: Free Press, 1967), 296.

# Resources for the Theospiritual Adventurer

Books on Celtic Christian spirituality abound, as part of the Celtic renaissance. Here are some that have inspired me over the years and that will inspire your own theospiritual adventures with Celtic spirituality and process theology.

de Waal, Esther. *The Celtic Vision.* Liguouri, 2001.

_____. *Every Earthly Blessing,* Moorehouse, 1999.

Epperly, Bruce. *The Center is Everywhere: Celtic Spirituality for a Postmodern World.* Parson's Porch, 2011.

_____. *The Mystic in You: Discovering a God-filled World.* Upper Room, 2018.

_____. *Process and Ministry.* Energion, 2018.

_____. *Process Spirituality: Practicing Holy Adventure.* Energion, 2017.

_____. *Process Theology: A Guide for the Perplexed.* Continuum, 2011.

_____. *Process Theology: Embracing Adventure with God.* Energion, 2014.

Farmer, Patricia Adams. *Embracing a Beautiful God.* Create Space, 2013.

_____. *Fat Soul: A Philosophy of S-I-Z-E.* Create Space, 2014.

_____. *The Metaphor Maker.* Create Space, 2009.

Keller, Catherine. *On the Mystery.* Fortress, 2008.

McDaniel, Jay. *Living from the Center.* Chalice, 2000.

McIntosh, Kenneth. *Water from Ancient Wells: Celtic Spirituality for Today.* Anamcara, 2011.

Newell, J. Philip. *The Book of Creation: An Introduction to Celtic Spirituality.* Paulist, 1999.

_____. *Christ of the Celts: The Healing of Creation.* Jossey-Bass, 2008.

_____. *Listening for the Heartbeat of God: A Celtic Spirituality.* Paulist, 1997.

Van de Weyer, Robert. *Celtic Fire: The Passionate Religious Vision of Ancient Britain and Ireland.* Doubleday, 1991.

# TOPICAL LINE DRIVES

## *Straight to the Point in under 44 Pages*

All Topical Line Drives volumes are priced at $5.99 print and $2.99 in all ebook formats.

## Available

| | |
|---|---|
| The Authorship of Hebrews: The Case for Paul | David Alan Black |
| What Protestants Need to Know about Roman Catholics | Robert LaRochelle |
| What Roman Catholics Need to Know about Protestants | Robert LaRochelle |
| Forgiveness: Finding Freedom from Your Past | Harvey Brown, Jr. |
| Process Theology: Embracing Adventure with God | Bruce Epperly |
| Holistic Spirituality | Bruce Epperly |
| To Date or Not to Date | D. Kevin Brown |
| The Eucharist: Encounters with Jesus at the Table | Robert D. Cornwall |
| The Authority of Scripture in a Postmodern Age | Robert D. Cornwall |
| Rendering unto Caesar | Chris Surber |
| The Caregiver's Beattitudes | Robert Martin |
| What is Wrong with Social Justice | Elgin Hushbeck, Jr. |
| I'm Right and You're Wrong | Steve Kindle |
| Words of Woe: Alternative Lectionary Texts | Robert D. Cornwall |
| Stewardship: God's Way of Recreating the World | Steve Kindle |
| Those Footnotes in Your New Testament | Thomas W. Hudgins |
| Jonah: When God Changes | Bruce G. Epperly |
| Ruth & Esther: Women of Agency and Adventure | Bruce G. Epperly |
| Constructing Your Testimony | Doris Horton Murdoch |
| Process Spirituality | Bruce Epperly |
| Process and Ministry | Bruce Epperly |
| To Be or Not To Be | David Moffett-Moore |

## Forthcoming

| | |
|---|---|
| God the Creator: The Variety of Christian Views on Origins | Henry Neufeld |

(The titles of planned volumes may change before release.)

Generous Quantity Discounts Available
Dealer Inquiries Welcome
Energion Publications — P.O. Box 841
Gonzalez, FL 32560
Website: http://energionpubs.com
Phone: (850) 525-3916

# MORE FROM ENERGION PUBLICATIONS

## Personal Study

| | | |
|---|---|---|
| Holy Smoke! Unholy Fire | Bob McKibben | $14.99 |
| The Jesus Paradigm | David Alan Black | $17.99 |
| When People Speak for God | Henry Neufeld | $17.99 |
| The Sacred Journey | Chris Surber | $11.99 |

## Christian Living

| | | |
|---|---|---|
| Faith in the Public Square | Robert D. Cornwall | $16.99 |
| Grief: Finding the Candle of Light | Jody Neufeld | $8.99 |
| Crossing the Street | Robert LaRochelle | $16.99 |
| Life in the Spirit | J. Hamilton Weston | $12.99 |

## Bible Study

| | | |
|---|---|---|
| Learning and Living Scripture | Lentz/Neufeld | $12.99 |
| Inspiration: Hard Questions, Honest Answers | Alden Thompson | $29.99 |
| Colossians & Philemon | Allan R. Bevere | $12.99 |
| Ephesians: A Participatory Study Guide | Robert D. Cornwall | $9.99 |

## Theology

| | | |
|---|---|---|
| Christian Archy | David Alan Black | $9.99 |
| The Politics of Witness | Allan R. Bevere | $9.99 |
| Ultimate Allegiance | Robert D. Cornwall | $9.99 |
| Angels, Mysteries, and Miracles | Bruce Epperly | $9.99 |
| The Journey to the Undiscovered Country | William Powell Tuck | $9.99 |
| Death, Immortality, and Resurrection | Edward W. H. Vick | $14.99 |
| Perseverance and Salvation | Alexander Stewart | $9.99 |

## Ministry

| | | |
|---|---|---|
| Clergy Table Talk | Kent Ira Groff | $9.99 |
| Thrive | Ruth Fletcher | $14.99 |
| Out of the Office: A Theology of Ministry | Bob Cornwall | $9.99 |

(The titles of planned volumes may change before release.)

Generous Quantity Discounts Available
Dealer Inquiries Welcome
Energion Publications — P.O. Box 841
Gonzalez, FL 32560
Website: http://energionpubs.com
Phone: (850) 525-3916

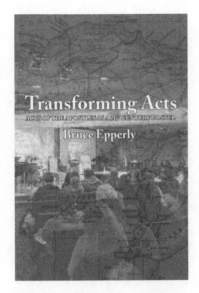

This book is an inspiration to
Christians in today's world!

**Rev. Shauna Hyde**, Pastor
author of *Fifty Shades of Grace* and
*Victim No More*

## BY BRUCE EPPERLY

[A] work of pastoral genius.

**Joel Watts**
UnsettledChristianity.com

CPSIA information can be obtained
at www.ICGtesting.com
Printed in the USA
BVHW031156190719
553928BV00001B/311/P